GW00832373

Getting Out

Personal Financial Planning to Successfully Exit the Owner Driven Business

Kathleen Adams CFP® CPWA®

Getting Out

Printed by:
90-Minute Books
302 Martinique Drive
Winter Haven, FL 33884
www.90minutebooks.com

Copyright © 2016, Kathleen Adams CFP® CPWA®

Published in the United States of America

Book ID: 151019-00261

ISBN-13: 978-0692652282
ISBN-10: 0692652280

No parts of this publication may be reproduced without correct attribution
to the author of this book.

For more information on 90-Minute Books including finding out how you can
publish your own lead generating book, visit www.90minutebooks.com or call
(863) 318-0464

Here's What's Inside…

"Planning is bringing the future into the present so you can do something about it now."-Alan Lakein

Introduction

After many years and hundreds of Financial Plans we believe that all business exit plans need to start with planning for the owner at a personal level.

People who have built a great business have put enormous time, energy, strategic planning and revenue toward its continual growth. They have taken risks and been through numerous ups and downs. It's rare that they've been able to put the same effort into their personal well-being for the future.

Owning an owner-driven business means the business is highly dependent on the owner which produces a unique set of challenges. With an owner-driven business, the owner has spent a great deal of his/her own time developing, funding, and working hands on to create a successful business. The owner is intimately involved in generating revenue, building relationships and managing staff and employees. Sometimes the demanding needs of the business mean that they forego thinking about their long-term personal financial situation. Their focus has always been on first class service to clients and the revenue it generates. They often end up investing everything they have back into the business to keep it going. Although they have enjoyed wonderful lifestyles because of their businesses, they haven't been able to think about how they are going to maintain that lifestyle when their business income stops, or even the best way to exit their company.

Part of the problem is there is a lot of crossover between the spending owners and families do when they run their own business. Looking ahead, they realize that revenue is going to stop or slow down, and they really don't know what to do about this. In fact, one of the mistakes we often see owners of owner-driven businesses make is thinking that since they have a growing business and increasing revenue, they have increased personal wealth outside of equity in the business. That's very often not the case.

I want business owners to think about how they are going to exit their business so it is a win-win for the business and their family. They have spent a lifetime growing and managing their business, and now they are looking toward the next phase. Whether it be a new opportunity or more time with family and friends, they start to realize that they don't have a strategy for how to get out of the business. After many years of working with these professionals it has become extremely clear that exiting an owner-driven service business is more difficult than just selling it, and very often strategies have to be put into place far in advance for it to be done right.

Enjoy the book!

I hope the book inspires you to think about life after your business and encourages you to begin the planning process so you can increase your sense of personal financial freedom when you exit your owner-driven business.

To Your Continued Success!

Kathleen Adams

*"Your life is controlled by
what you focus on"
– Tony Robbins*

Why Don't More Owner-Driven Businesses Have Solid Exit Plans?

Why don't more owner-driven businesses have solid exit plans in place when they go to transition out of the business? Business owners are smart; so why don't they have this piece handled?

Sometimes it's simply a matter of time; especially for the owner-driven business. Connected to that is lack of expertise and education in this area. Combine those two and it's easy to see why this might fall to the bottom of the list of priorities. Since people who created their own business have often done it mostly alone and made all the decisions, they typically are not used to asking for advice.

Even if they are ready to get advice on this subject, where do they begin? Their tax advisor who helped them incorporate? Their attorney who drafted the partnership agreement? Or maybe the business broker who can help them value the business and make suggestions that would enhance a sale?

I believe the very best way to get started is by understanding what the business exit means to you personally, financially and mentally. If you create a vision of the outcome you want, it will be a great guide to strategizing the type of exit you need and want.

This is where reality sets in. It's often very difficult to put a significant or a legitimate valuation on what the business might be worth because it's owner-driven. They don't really know what they have, what it would sell for, or if it's sellable because of the fact that it is owner-driven. They think their business is possibly unsellable because anyone purchasing it would be concerned that the business is not viable without the owner staying in it. They fear the key relationships would be lost when the owner leaves, especially if the business offers a type of service based on the owner's expertise. It is difficult to see how to replace that.

Our process is well suited for owners across various industries; such as professional firms (accountants, attorneys, medical/dental groups, etc.) to those in distribution, technology, manufacturing, etc. You take out the long-term relationships built into those different industries or the expertise of the top designer or doctor and it may be legitimately difficult to sell, merge or create a succession plan. You can't guarantee revenue is going to continue when the person who has created and maintained the relationships steps away.

Other owners feel, *"I'll just work until I die. I love what I do. I'll just stay in."* Or they haven't had time to think about it because they are working so hard in that business and revenue is good; they are not thinking about what-ifs down the road. They don't stop and look around the corner to when this cash flow is going to stop. We know that life changes continually and often changes quickly. An unexpected health event can knock everything off course. Planning around this uncertainty is crucial.

Another factor that impacts exit planning is family members or long time employees who would be affected if they leave. Perhaps the owner has identified someone to take over the business when they exit someday, although there is no proper succession plan in place for that.

Sometimes they believe that since business has been doing so well that it's crazy to start thinking about an exit when they can just keep growing the business, enjoy the income, and then sell for higher value.

What's concerning in today's economic environment is that many of these owner-driven businesses, such as professional service firms, are being commoditized through corporate owned entities, internet services, or there is simply an excess of them getting ready to be sold as boomers get older. When we look at this situation we see it's becoming harder to generate revenue, at least at the same high level. Sometimes the owners are quite simply getting tired of the pressure on pricing for their services.

The motivation isn't where it was 20 years ago, or 10 years ago, and that is having an emotional effect on them. In fact, that's usually when they come to see me. I would prefer it was sooner. They usually come to us when they have a few years left and suddenly they need that personal financial strategy because they don't have a considerable amount of time or business revenues still to come. That is when this planning becomes crucial.

Ideally what we want to do is get in front of people prior to going into full panic mode a few years before they see the business shutting down or revenue drying up. We want to be there ahead of time and help them build a personal vision that can integrate with the overall vision for the business. Ultimately they should end up with the flexibility to know it is okay to step away and exit in five or ten years' time.

If you think of Exiting an Owner Driven Business into a successful retirement as a game, such as a football game, what might be missing is the head coach. The business owner owns the team, but he typically doesn't coach it or play in it. We are committed to operating as the head coach – adding our experience as well as expertise to the owner's intelligence and success. We bring professional, objective advice, help form the team, consistently evaluate the players and the strategies along with making appropriate adjustments as circumstances change. We have already created our trademarked process, **The Owner's Plan**®, to facilitate the *special* kind of personal planning needed for the owner-driven business.

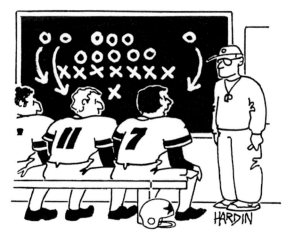

"Excuse me, Coach — But are we the hugs or the Kisses?"

*"Investing time in yourself is
the only safe investment that
will give you maximum
return throughout life."*
- Kamari aka Lyrikal

Shifting Focus to Building Wealth Outside of the Business

For business owners, what does creating a strategy for replacing their income when they are ready to transition out of their business really mean?

Owners often correlate a successful and profitable business to personal wealth. Often times it almost works in the opposite way; increased revenue allows higher personal spending (which is often paid directly through the business in the form of travel and entertainment). In addition to lifestyle expenses, big expenses such as college educations need to be covered through this revenue. It's also common to see the desire for substantial home improvements or second homes, which may also cause additional debt.

Many times owners have set up retirement plans as advised by their tax advisor and have been funding those consistently, which is great. Many have substantial equity as their homes have appreciated in value through the years. However, we rarely see an escalating personal wealth building strategy that goes along with increasing business profitability.

When they retire, they won't be getting a pension. There is no company benefit beyond themselves, so they have to build enough wealth to create an income stream which will last a lifetime and take care of their lifestyle, oftentimes for themselves and potentially their spouse and family. That's a big, tall job, and it means that they have to shift some of the focus away from their current lifestyle and reinvesting in the growth of the business to building some wealth outside of it. This is the wealth that isn't at the mercy of business performance. It can definitely be done, especially in their high income-earning years with the right strategy in place.

We want to transform business owners' personal financial anxiety into excitement and energy for their future with a big focus on providing the ability to enjoy their lives. It's about having the freedom to stay in the business, if they love what they do, but not be obligated to it for a lifetime due to financial needs.

We have heard hundreds of times, *"I love this business, and will be in it for the rest of my life."* Could it also be that they know they cannot live comfortably without that business revenue? This process should help them turbocharge their business, because they have clarity over what it needs to do for them on the personal side.

Now they can either begin building their own personal wealth with a purpose or optimize what they already have to support their most important goals. We have seen that people who created their own businesses usually have a need for new goals, even after they retire. Those need to be paid for as well.

"Strategic Planning is Worthless – Unless there is first a strategic vision." -
John Naisbitt

Game Plan for Getting Out: The Owner's Plan®

Strategy #1: Discovery

Discovery is the first critical step in the process; we can't provide proper direction unless we know more about what you - our client really wants.

You may have an immediate need to be addressed such as college funding for high school children or you are getting ready to buy a much bigger home and have concerns regarding fluctuating business income. Or perhaps there is an offer from an outside source or a partner that wants to buy your business and you have no idea if it makes sense to take it.

We want to understand all of the financial issues that are important to you or keeping you up at night.

We also want to ask: What does the future look like when you are ready to or forced to step away from this business?

Even if you enjoy your work, what would your future hold if you knew you didn't need that business income in order to maintain your lifestyle?

You might say you want to prioritize enjoyment of your wealth and are ok if you run out of money on the day you die. Or you may feel strongly about enjoying your new found freedom but want to make sure there is a legacy for your family. These are very different goals. All of it matters.

This step sets the direction for the whole plan. We prioritize, create scenarios around the top 2-3 visions, and identify what can be put into action steps for the near-term (typically 1-3 years).

Reality has shown us that if you try to count on things that are 20 years away as if they are set in stone, you are most likely doomed.

It's much better to prepare for the future, expect adjustments, and continue taking immediate positive actions.

Strategy #2: Understand Your Lifestyle Costs

For this strategy, we want to identify the costs that the business is carrying. Once we identify that cost, we can start to understand what you want to continue to spend. This strategy is not just identifying the actual numbers, but knowing how you want to live and what you need to plan for in the future.

We start with the notion that we need to simplify the complexity around the usual crossover between business and personal expenses. Gaining this clarity is extremely important.

Every owner that I know, including myself, pays for things through the business which are still considered personal expenses or will turn into personal expenses after exiting the business. These are legitimate, but what happens over time is that you don't realize just how much is really going through that business compared to what you are using as take-home pay for yourself.

That's the first step. Simplify and create great clarity around your real cash flow.

When we sit down we will discuss your vision for your lifestyle going into retirement, including the desire for increasing lifestyle spending. (While we have had some clients say they are going to reduce their lifestyle we have yet to see that come to fruition and we are very hesitant to plan around that assumption.)

Fully understanding all current lifestyle costs is the foundation for high-level planning in terms of distribution income.

We have worked with many, many business owners who are considerably off in what they think they are spending against what they are actually spending – usually underestimating by 25–40%, which can be a considerable differential.

Examples include cell phones, internet, cars, eating out, travel, health insurance, gifts, and occasionally, they have some payroll for their high school and college-age children. These are some of the items the business rightfully pays for but need to be factored into the personal side when they exit the business.

A lot of business owners do charitable contributions. Business owners are taxed astronomically, so they do it through the business, but most of the time they want to continue giving to charity throughout their lifetimes. The ability to continue giving charitably needs to be maintained.

This is about looking forward versus just staying in the present. What we want you to do is look forward, look around the corner. You may do it for the business, but not for yourself personally.

By looking forward, you get the big picture, and from there we can look at scenarios. So let's say that something as simple as, *"I really want to buy a second place in Hawaii"* or, *"I want to help my children buy a home,"* can actually be looked at in the context of what-if scenarios in your plans. Looking forward really helps you create a better future.

Strategy #3: Where Do You Stand?

This strategy is when we sit down and analyze what you have already done to build wealth outside the business and the amount of profitability that is available to direct towards your personal goals.

If you have a buyer or a succession plan that is in place, we use those numbers to evaluate how well that will fund the income needs that we have calculated. We have to take a very careful look at that, because our purpose now is to consider how we can help build the kind of wealth you need to finance the future you just envisioned during Strategy #1 and #2. In some cases, we will need to adjust to what will be realistically available to finance the future.

At this point, if not already done, it may be necessary to get professional advice on a valuation for the business and its potential for a sale, merger or succession buy-out. This will give us an initial idea, if nothing changes, what to expect.

It's much better to know ahead of time whether or not we can count on this business asset to help support the personal goals after the exit. With clarity around what you already have, what the gaps are, and what we are going to need to do, we can identify next steps.

We will analyze the investments and do a huge amount of risk assessment with you. We believe that's another neglected area because the financial world will not be able to rely on past returns for a variety of reasons; the projections we do need to be very realistic and forward thinking.

We have incorporated new software and processes into this analysis because we need to know what your comfort level is.

If you have built your wealth in either the market or in real estate, you have a comfort level with risk that has seen dramatic shifts not only through price volatility, but also the volatility of your business performance and your proximity towards exiting it.

We need to know what that is so you don't make big mistakes in the future. This is when people often take the biggest risks to try to catch up and "make a killing".

At this stage, we are analyzing and strategizing for what we need to fund; what amount of wealth do we want to strive for?

By the way, we are big believers in diversifying wealth and sources of income whenever possible. That means not relying totally on any one asset class, such as the stock market or bond ladders or real estate. We love passive income, and we love real estate. We believe that you can build wealth in a variety of ways. What we are recommending is to know where you are at versus where you need to be before you make future investing decisions.

"Accountability separates the wishers in life from the action-takers that care enough about their future to account for their daily actions." John Di Lemme.

Strategy #4 Establishing and Maintaining a Goal-Based Investing Plan

Since investments will ultimately be funding your future after the business, it is essential that they are positioned with your goals in mind and in a manner that will keep you from making big mistakes during the best and worst of times. Your plan needs to include a complete analysis of how you are currently invested. That's why we use the software we described above.

With regard to the risk analysis, I think the biggest mistake financial advisors make in our industry is that they are focused on percentage returns. You know, if you are with a bunch of financial advisors over lunch, we would say, *"Oh, the S&P is down 1%,"* or, when we would meet with clients, we might say, *"Oh, well, the market's down 10%, but your portfolio is only down 5%."* What we have realized is that when you are doing risk analysis, it is crucial to focus as much or maybe more on the actual dollar amounts.

Most business owners don't think of things in percentages, you think in dollars. What happens with a lot of business owners is you build personal wealth toward the end of your career, so when retirement comes, you have a pretty significant amount invested, whether it be in real estate or in the market.

Suddenly, a 10% drop on $5 million is $500,000. That's a lot of money, and probably not an amount of money you have seen a portfolio drop by before. When we do risk analysis, we are focusing on total dollar amounts and dollar volatility because we want to look at the bottom line – not at percentages against a benchmark or percentages against an index.

Another problem we see is that many clients have had success by investing in one area. We've seen people with excellent wealth in real estate but it's not able to give them enough rental income to support their needs. It could also be the case that a big mortgage creates more risk in retirement. Or perhaps there is no mortgage but they've owned the property for 25 years and won't sell it because of the major tax consequences.

We can use strategies but it will involve tradeoffs and willingness to be flexible.

If you plan proactively on how real estate will enhance your future goals, you will make better decisions on how much of your wealth should be in one asset class.

Another example is you may be able to purchase your current office building or be looking for a new location to buy. With proper tax and business planning, and manageable debt, that office might be best owned separately from the business so when the business is sold it can be leased back to the new owner for passive income.

The bottom line is there is no free lunch in investing; every time you grow wealth risk is present in some form and you will always feel better if you are proactively planning for your next step.

Making realistic growth projections on your invested financial assets are also key elements in the planning process, because 99.9% of the time, planning relies upon getting growth from the assets you have.

It's crucial to know exactly how much risk you are willing to take so that you can plan around the amount of return that could potentially give and the amount of volatility it will provide. It's not just in investments; it's also in real estate and other areas, so it's crucial to factor that in.

We believe that planning using past performance on assets can be problematic and create problems in later life. Can we honestly say that Bonds will perform in the next 30 years as they did in the last? It's very unlikely. Projected conservative returns should be used instead.

Finance has shown us that human beings are hardwired to be horrible investors. We're just terrible investors by nature. We operate on instinct and fear is the strongest emotion. That's scientific fact. Greed is also a big one.

The best thing we have done in the last ten years is helped people not make some very big mistakes. By doing that, we've added enormous value. We have specific strategies to use with goal based investing that include creating proper cash accounts, adjusting allocations to align with time frame for a certain portfolio and having rules for taking income during market declines.

You don't put together a strategy and an action plan without accountability. We don't just give you a plan and then let you go off into the sunset and assume you are going to execute it. It's really about deadlines, following up, and being accountable. It's about working with your other advisors or introducing you to ones as needed.

Progress has to be monitored as we've never pretended we can predict the future with our plans; we cannot know exactly what inflation or taxes or markets will throw our way. So we continually make course corrections and adjustments but we are always doing so with the end game in mind.

This isn't a one-time relationship. It's a constant relationship over time. That is where we go with the next steps and it becomes a consultative relationship where we are updating the plan, tracking the plan, and making sure we are progressing in the right way, and if we aren't, we make the necessary switches or strategy changes.

We're like a financial GPS—if you go off course, we will redirect you and get you back on track.

"It's cheaper than a personal trainer and twice as motivating."

Strategy #5: Interactive Decision-Making

Our next strategy is what we call interactive decision-making. This involves using high-level software where we can play out the future based on either your current financial situation or projected financial situation. Then, with our software, we can sit down and go through how each decision or each goal you want to achieve affects your retirement, longevity, and cash flow.

This is powerful because you can see it happening in front of your eyes. We use a complex statistical analysis called Monte Carlo which incorporates risk and volatility of investments, whether they are stocks and bonds or real estate. We can factor all that in and show our clients the probability of success.

We can show you how every decision you make and everything you want to do—whether it's to buy a boat, purchase a condo in Hawaii, or spend an extra $80,000 on travel—affects future financial success. Once we have gone through all of these options, and you can see how feasible it all is, we go to the next step, which is putting together an action plan and a strategy for getting you to where you want to be as efficiently as possible.

The great thing about this part is all the technical analysis and all of that is in the background. It's available for you to see in print if you want, but we like to make the meetings very efficient and engaging so you can sit down with us and we can say, *"We're going to push this button, and we're going to add in that second home. Now let's look at the graph and see how it affected your success in retirement."* Then we can take the home out and add in some extra travel.

We're doing the what-ifs and going back and forth. We will <u>not</u> step behind a curtain and come back with a big plan and say, "Here's what you need to do."

You, and your spouse if applicable, will be involved so you can make choices for yourselves, and then we will plan around what you decide is best for you.

We call this interactive decision-making. We can't use strategy and action items without you first having clarity about how these different scenarios look and how realistic they are. We don't have a problem telling you if your assumptions are way off because it's only going to benefit you in the future, and strategy is a lot more efficient when we plan around attainable goals. This meeting really puts us all on the same page.

This is an excellent way to make sure that we are working together. Back to our analogy, the owner of the football team respects strategic decisions made by the head coach, perhaps his defensive and offensive coordinators, on acquiring players. However, as the owner, he needs to evaluate the pros and cons of these actions and agree upon the final outcome.

For more information on the software we use click or type into your web browser:

https://vimeo.com/79134329

Strategy #6: Where Are the Red Flags?

The next strategy is looking for the things you are not thinking about, things that could seriously derail even the best of plans. Usually these are events that are not necessarily probable, but certainly possible. Often people are very, very busy and they are not thinking about the things which could really blow up their future.

We take a deep look at the obvious.

What would happen if you were in an accident and unable to go into work tomorrow? We need to have a crisis action plan in place. It's more than insurance.

How would everything transfer? It is about looking at who is the first person you call, especially in the owner-driven business. It's looking at, *"Does somebody have passwords to my computer?"*

We look at worst case scenarios and the best ways to protect the family. What are the things we can put in place, and who are the other people we need to bring in to look at the red flags and inefficiencies?

At that step, you don't know what you don't know. Even though we cannot prevent or manage all of the "red flags", even having a "first person to call" can be enormously helpful and take away much anxiety.

Sometimes red flags are as simple as inefficiencies that can be corrected. We see something where we are quite certain a different kind of tax strategy could be helpful, so we will consult with the tax advisor. We don't give tax advice, but we plan toward it. We will sit down and see if we can improve inefficiencies where you haven't seen them.

You may also have the ability to protect yourself financially, so we examine the cost of protection in relation to all of their spending needs and execute if all looks good.

For example...

We know a great couple and a self-made success story. They have done well, saved well, and we just helped them optimize how they would take their income. Before they met us, they did not have a proper plan in place, and they hadn't thought about the potential excess cost of long-term care. They are both healthy individuals, but they had seen other people who have been hit with health issues and the drain it put on their finances. We ran a what-if scenario and we put in long-term care costs just to test the wealth they have and see how well-funded they are. It was fairly disruptive not only to

*their future lifestyle but to the legacy they wanted to
leave for their children.*

*This is why we recommended a strategy to protect
against long-term health care costs. They had the
liquidity to do it, so it worked out well for them. They
believed it was important. That was about two
years ago, and this year, the wife was diagnosed
with MS. She is only in her early 60's, so the
chance of them having to use this long-term care is
now huge, and she's already walking with pain,
potentially not able to use stairs at some point.
Their benefits of over $600,000 are going to be
available to help her stay comfortably in her home
and have home health care without an immediate
impact on their wealth. That is really important to
us, and it highlights how important it is to discover
and see what options we have to manage the red
flags.*

With all of our clients, we believe that it's important
for us to have a relationship with your other
advisory team members. We work far more
proficiently and deal with potential issues so much
better when we have a relationship with your tax
advisor, estate planner, business consultant, etc. If
you have that team and the spouse knows the team
and they have been a part of the planning process,
there's so much more clarity, and it's far more
efficient, so we find that's crucial, this intentional
team formation. (You'll see a chapter on this later).

Strategy #7: Portfolio Distribution Blueprint

The last piece is to look at everything we have put together and answer the big question: *"How are we going to take steps to replace the business income? What is that going to look like in the future?"* At this point, we have done a lot of planning. We need to drill down into, *"Are we going to have real estate? Are we going to have passive income from the business? Are we going to have mostly money from retirement plans or are we going to have trust accounts set up? Do we count on social security and if yes, when should it start?"*

We're going to now put all the pieces together because the big question for us is typically, *"How do I now distribute this wealth? How do I incorporate all the income sources and tap into all the wealth I've created to now make it all support me the way I want to be supported?"* We see the wealthiest of people who have loaded their net worth in terrific real estate, but they have no idea now how to make that work to support them.

As we stated earlier, often, unless you started very, very early, net rental incomes are not going to give you the high six-figure income you want during retirement. So, we have to look at a lot of strategy around real estate.

If you have the potential to sell your business or have a succession plan, then revenue will come from that. However, if we determine your business is done when the owner leaves, then we are going to try to maximize it like crazy for the rest of the time it has. You are going to make sure that a certain amount of the profits continually builds wealth outside of that business for when you leave.

We put a very specific system in place for our clients, creating a diagram that shows how we're going to set the income stream the day the business revenue stops.

What this leads to is a process we don't believe anyone else is doing, which is our Portfolio Distribution Blueprint. Most advisors just recommend the 4% rule of thumb for distribution. This simply isn't tailored well enough or specifically enough to the individual or family. This model is somewhat outdated, and it just isn't as relevant anymore. There has been a lot of historical research which, at one time, was a very good approach, but now there is additional important research and it needs to be applied in a forward thinking way. One of the biggest reasons is the theory assumed certain historical rates of return which most likely won't be the same in the future; especially for people retiring in the next 5-10 years.

For example, a common recommendation is "You can withdraw 4% from your portfolio and you'll be okay with inflation." It's not a safe way of projecting out income and how much you can distribute; it just became an easy way to plan to take money from the portfolios. Individuals began to think they could manage the income plans themselves due to this simple method that has been highlighted in the media for over 20 years.

The problem is even the 4% rule has requirements that most people ignore or don't realize in regard to how the portfolio needs to be set up. In addition, there is the problem of evaluating the expectation for returns in the current economic environment compared with when that percentage was researched.

The first thing to understand, before you even get into what the percentage is, is what do you want? Some of our clients want a very safe and constant income, and they just want the same amount every year that grows with inflation for the rest of their lives. They have shown us they can stick to it, which is important as well. They want it, and they mean it, and they are much happier knowing they have a constant and it's not going to run out.

Some clients want to optimize their income now for the next 10 to 15 years. They want to go out and enjoy the next 10 to 15 years and are prepared to accept less income later in life, as long as they are protected on their health care side, which is one of the red flags I talked about earlier.

Once you understand that, then that's the first part of the process. Some clients will be prepared to accept less income when markets are rocky and valuations are down, and we can adapt. Maybe they will take one less vacation or something like that. Other clients are not prepared to accept less income. So, in our Portfolio Distribution Blueprint, these are the questions we ask. We also ask whether real estate will be accessible to us in terms of equity in the home. Can we rely on them selling one of their properties down the road?

For example...

We had a client with three properties: they are just completing a very large estate in Montana, they have a completed home in Nevada, and they have a home in Southern California. We were very surprised to find out, as we were doing the blueprint questionnaire, that the one they definitely didn't want to sell was the little one-story in California because they had determined it would be their go-to spot when their health got bad. They could stay in it because it has no stairs and the maintenance is easy. By understanding that, we get permission to plan around a sale of another property in the future because they have a lot of equity right now in real estate. We have an agreement on which one would go first, what time frame, and if they want to keep it at least ten years.

We know none of this is set in stone, but we have to give them a realistic blueprint of spending, and real estate considerations are always a part of it.

For this to be successful, we have to stay with them. We have to have that ongoing commitment to monitor and update accountability. Toward that end, we provide our clients with software that consolidates all of their accounts because they usually have accounts at different institutions—real estate, mortgages across the board—and so we provide a consolidated software so they can track it all through one log-in. We can update a plan when need be, or we can update it if there's some big financial decision they are making and we want to look at their progress, or if we're just doing the annual check-up, as we call it, to review where they are currently.

That's all part of that ongoing process, but the two great things about that are 1) it simplifies the complexity of their life and their wealth because we can get in there and all see it in one place, and 2) it makes it much easier for us to monitor and update. So, should something happen midstream, which is not uncommon—something hits the business, cash flow stops, a client dies unexpectedly and everything is going bad—our team and the client's family have a lot of information from that software so we can sit down and say, *"Okay, where are we at and what are our next steps at this point?"*

Along with considering all of these areas in relation to exiting the business, we also know there are some owners that feel very confident that no planning is needed because they have either saved substantial wealth or have had a big purchase offer. *"I can just put my $5 million profit into muni bonds and live off the 5% interest. No big tax worries and no market worries."*

Here's the problem, the $250,000 interest you can live on when retirement starts may be fine for your spending needs. However in 10 years, at 3% average inflation, you will need about $336,000 just to live the same life. Also, if excess money is needed, you may be required to sell a bond at the wrong economic time and be forced to sell at a loss. Not to mention your $5 million won't be growing much if at all as you are taking all of the income.

And what if a great opportunity comes along that you want to participate in? Do you take the risk and compromise the income stream? If you want to help your grandchildren with college education costs, how do you know the amount that is safe to offer them? You don't even know how many grandkids you may have!

The bottom line is it's important to play the retirement income game all the way through with a well-thought out strategy that can be adjusted when needed no matter how well you have done while working. If you have had a fantastic first half in football, up 27-0, it's doubtful that you relax and forget about competing during the 2nd half of the game. You may be focusing more on defense during that half, but you do not let your guard down and assume you have won when there is so much time left.

Bad Al

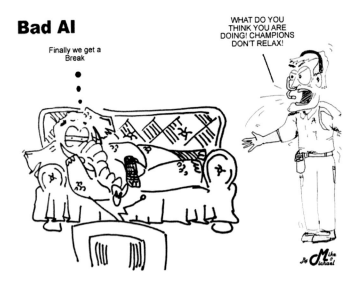

WHAT DO YOU THINK YOU ARE DOING! CHAMPIONS DON'T RELAX!

Finally we get a Break

Identifying the Intentional Team

A lot of times, people think they have a team because they have been working with an insurance agent and a CPA and maybe a banker, but oftentimes it's not a team at all because the right hand doesn't know what the left hand is doing. Sometimes various advisors are very protective of the category they are dealing with and everything's driven by tax or everything's driven by insurance, so we like to come in as the objective advocate for the clients at this stage and say, *"We have a very good intentional team because the intent is on how we can help this owner succeed. It's not about us."*

In some cases, there is a need to add new professional advisors because the owner has been working on their own and doing very well but recognized that it might be time for professional advice.

For example...

We have a client who came to us for personal planning. He is a young, successful business owner who was getting ready to expand his business operations by increasing his team and potentially his office space. He wanted to know if he would be taking on too much personal risk for himself by spending his profits on the business and didn't know how to manage what he wanted personally as well as professionally. Although his workload had been increasing because the business grew rapidly due to his excellent service, we could see that it was a critical time for outside professional help so he had appropriate guidance as he made these big decisions.

We suggested he consult with a business advisor. After interviewing them, he chose one that ultimately streamlined and guided his next steps. The cost was manageable and he found tremendous value from them, as did we. In addition, we felt that his retirement plan should be evaluated as well as his business entity, so he consulted with a qualified tax advisor.

We coordinated our efforts and now know how to plan around more realistic future business revenue that can be used for his personal wealth goals without disrupting the goals for the business.

Another client was in the process of selling his practice to his younger associate. As we were looking at the assets available for his future income stream without the business, we determined that there might be some issues with the structure of the current sale and financing. We worked with his very experienced and knowledgeable tax advisor who adjusted certain aspects of the sale, creating a better tax situation and an income stream through the sale. It was a win/win for the buyer and the seller – ultimately creating a much better retirement scenario for the seller.

We have great respect for the advisors that have helped our clients through the years and our main goal is to make sure that we can coordinate efforts to optimize the big decisions and actions that need to be taken. As illustrated, if extra advice is needed, we have spent many years finding great resources in case there is a need for additional help. The more proactively we can do that, the better.

Some of our favorite situations have been when we have determined that the financial foundation that fully supports an owner's income needs is complete, and there are assets left over to enjoy for opportunities they may have never considered before. It is exhilarating to show people that they can share their wealth with their children or grandchildren *now*, rather than after they are gone.

Our Decision Center allows us to show clients exactly how gifting now affects their financial future. It also allows us to explore the most efficient way possible to do this. We have great strategies for helping with this process without destroying a work ethic or creating entitlement. There are excellent resources we can bring to the table who can show them methods for bringing the family together to use some of their wealth to help others. We can coordinate some of these activities with tax and legal advisors to make sure we are optimizing the situation for the owner as well as his heirs or beneficiaries.

Lastly, teams are rarely static. Certain members are core people and likely to be together a long time, like your CPA, estate attorney, and hopefully your personal planning advisor. Additional members can be brought in as needed, including M&A professionals, insurance agents, mortgage brokers, etc.

The Owner's Plan® is designed to help create the purpose and the focus for team strategy, so the owner's personal needs are integrated with what the business is doing. Having a team only makes sense if there is a great mix of talent all intent on serving the best and most important goals of the owner.

©Glenn and Gary McCoy/Distributed by Universal Uclick via CartoonStock.com

> *"Success occurs when opportunity meets preparation." - Zig Ziglar*

Planning for a Successful Exit of Your Owner-Driven Business

As you can see from this book, we firmly believe all successful exits start with substantial personal planning for the owner in addition to the business.

Start with financial clarity and an understanding of what it will take to build what we call the personal financial foundation. Our process, The Owner's Plan®, specifically focuses on developing the personal financial foundation as the first step towards funding your essential and lifestyle needs with or without the business revenue. That means you will have complete clarity around what you want to spend and how you will finance that. It will give you great peace of mind.

With that foundation comes a feeling of confidence knowing that you and your family are secure, and a feeling of joy that your hard work has paid off and you can now keep doing it because you love it. Your professional goals will be turbo charged because they are integrated with your most important personal goals. Ultimately, you should have the freedom to continue building a bigger or better business, planning for an exit to this business under your own terms, or even starting a new one without guilt or worry, because you are not compromising your personal financial needs.

Because you now know what you need from the business, you will know which direction to take for your exit plan. This will require the expertise of your tax advisor and a business advisor who are willing to collaborate regarding the exit options you have available and the best way to enhance the personal financial foundation.

If you are still enjoying work and the profitability is growing, it's a perfect time to evaluate a future sale or potential succession plan. This is the time to consult with a business advisor who can offer proactive advice as to how to make your business more valuable or avoid activities that are making it less valuable.

If the practice has taken a downturn, it's time to strategize with professionals to determine if there is an alternative to an outright sale or if you simply need to maximize the remaining revenue years for the benefit of building personal wealth.

If there is an employee or family member who is being groomed to take over the business, now is the time to create professional strategy with your tax, legal and business advisors. We have a surprising number of creative strategies that can be used in succession planning if arranged early enough.

In all of these scenarios, you want to make sure that you are integrating the tax, legal, and business advice with your personal planning.

It's amazing how different the success of an exit is when the owner is first armed with knowledge regarding his personal financial requirements and uses that knowledge to guide the next steps, proactively whenever possible.

Ultimately, you need your own personal strategic plan for the future and partners to help you execute it, one that operates with a 'GPS' mentality, because course corrections will be inevitable. Adjustments will need to be made, just like in your business. We developed a platform of services and strategic partners for precisely this reason. Our services will grow to meet future planning after your foundation is funded.

If your exit has resulted in a highly profitable sale or revenue stream, this may require working with family wealth transfer issues that can happen as substantial wealth is achieved. These plans help identify an appropriate amount of funds available after your personal foundation needs are met that can be used for opportunities you will have once you leave your current business, such as surprisingly enjoyable philanthropic strategies.

The benefit of working together towards this end will be peace of mind. When you take control of things that you can control, you should feel a greater sense of freedom to enjoy your wealth now and perhaps even the ability to share some of your wealth during your lifetime rather than through an estate plan after you are gone.

The gift we want to give our clients is a wake-up call to prepare for the future so you can enjoy living in the present with clarity and confidence.

"If you have a high evaluation of yourself then your ability to recognize new facts is weakened."
-Robert M. Pirsig

The Owner's Scorecard

We've created an assessment to help you understand your current mindset towards your business and financial life.

If you already know you want some help at this point, we're always more than happy to sit down and have a free conversation.

If, after taking the assessment you now feel that the time might be right to explore your options please call our office at 310-712-2322.

It is essential to talk to us if you think you need help. Taking the brief assessment will definitely give you more clarity.

Mindset: Entrepreneurial

The risk and cost of owning your own business has made you want to focus on the simplest way to get out.	**1** **2** **3**
You enjoy owning your own business and have been frustrated with its slow progress toward profitability.	**4** **5** **6**
You have created a successful business and are not sure if any dramatic improvements are possible or needed since life is very comfortable.	**7** **8** **9**
Despite your success you often think about ways to improve your work and potential new opportunities to explore.	**10** **11** **12**

Score:

Mindset: Clarity	
You don't worry about the relationship between your personal and business spending since it's all your income anyway.	1
	2
	3
You know your business is paying for many personal expenses but don't see why it's important to evaluate at this time.	4
	5
	6
Your business pays for legitimate personal expenses and it might be helpful to understand these numbers for the future in retirement.	7
	8
	9
You want complete clarity on what is being spent to support you and your family so you know what it takes to maintain your lifestyle.	10
	11
	12

	Score:	

Mindset: Futuristic	
You take things day to day and can't look ahead at this point because increasing competition and commoditization are the priority.	1
	2
	3
You have a future vision for the success of your business but do not really see a need for a personal vision that integrates with it.	4
	5
	6
Your vision for your business is leading to increasing success/wealth so you assume your personal wealth is growing which will enable a great future.	7
	8
	9
You desire to know that you are maximizing your current activities to achieve personal future goals, dreams and financial freedom.	10
	11
	12

Score:	

Mindset: Confidence	
It's too overwhelming to worry about your personal wealth when your business profitability is still so challenging.	1
	2
	3
You do have some anxiety around how you are managing your growing wealth but have been too busy and nervous to actually take action.	4
	5
	6
You are satisfied with how your current wealth is positioned both personally and professionally but might be open to an objective review.	7
	8
	9
You are committed to reviewing and improving your personal as well as professional wealth building strategies.	10
	11
	12

Score:

Mindset: Collaborative

You are very self-directed and don't need outside professional advice for your business or your personal life.	1
	2
	3
You utilize professional advice only when essential, i.e. legal document; tax filing, etc.	4
	5
	6
You are open to using professional advisors but don't know who to bring in next as often times you have mostly relied on one.	7
	8
	9
You understand the benefit of professional advice and having a coordinated, trusted team ready to help you.	10
	11
	12

Score:

Mindset: Strategic	
You can't imagine life without your business so no need to strategize for life beyond the business.	1 2 3
You do not see the need for building a plan around replacing business income when the business is doing well and you plan to work a long time.	4 5 6
Your business has grown substantially and you assume that it will be sold for a lump sum that you will use for spending as needed.	7 8 9
You are building wealth and want an exit strategy to identify how you will replace your income stream without your business.	10 11 12

	Score:	

Mindset: Responsibility	
Personal financial security for you and your family is important but you are building the business for that reason.	1
	2
	3
You have taken some steps to protect your loved ones and business but often worry that it's not enough or it's outdated.	4
	5
	6
You relied on different advisors to help you look at managing your exposure to personal plus professional risk and feel you've done enough.	7
	8
	9
You want confidence that your family is financially secure and your business will survive in the event of your death or full disability.	10
	11
	12

Score:

Mindset: Accountability	
	1
You operate on a day to day basis and don't need accountability from planning.	2
	3
You utilize a business plan for goals and monitor progress but haven't had the time, desire, or expertise to create personal plan yet.	4
	5
	6
You have your own plan for future financial needs but do not have accountability or an action plan professionally designed for you.	7
	8
	9
You desire goals, strategy, and accountability to maximize success personally as well as professionally.	10
	11
	12

Score:

The Owner's Scorecard

Mindset		
	Entrepreneurial	
	Clarity	
	Futuristic	
	Confidence	
	Collaborative	
	Strategic	
	Responsible	
	Focus	

Score:	

Score	What It Means
0-47	At this point, you might not see the need, or have the time to devote to a personal planning process that includes professional advice. If you do decide you want to take success to the next level, feel free to call to discuss or get started on your own first step which is clarifying what you actually want the business to do for you.
48-96	You have started to recognize the need or have actually started planning around what it will take to have personal financial security once your business ends. Whether you are in the first stages of considering what it will take to exit your business, or are well into the strategy toward it, call us to see how The Owner's Plan® can help.

35963237R00036

Made in the USA
San Bernardino, CA
09 July 2016